To Dear Sue,

with every good wish

love

Douglas

Poetry Matters – Write!

(What you don't know CAN hurt you)

Douglas McCulloch

authorHOUSE®

AuthorHouse™ UK
1663 Liberty Drive
Bloomington, IN 47403 USA
www.authorhouse.co.uk
Phone: UK TFN: 0800 0148641 (Toll Free inside the UK)
UK Local: (02) 0369 56322 (+44 20 3695 6322 from outside the UK)

© 2024 Douglas McCulloch. All rights reserved.

No part of this book may be reproduced, stored in a retrieval system, or transmitted by any means without the written permission of the author.

Published by AuthorHouse   07/11/2024

ISBN: 979-8-8230-8861-9 (sc)
ISBN: 979-8-8230-8862-6 (e)

Library of Congress Control Number: 2024913519

Print information available on the last page.

Any people depicted in stock imagery provided by Getty Images are models, and such images are being used for illustrative purposes only.
Certain stock imagery © Getty Images.

This book is printed on acid-free paper.

Because of the dynamic nature of the Internet, any web addresses or links contained in this book may have changed since publication and may no longer be valid. The views expressed in this work are solely those of the author and do not necessarily reflect the views of the publisher, and the publisher hereby disclaims any responsibility for them.

Douglas is a writer. He was the first of his family to go to university full-time (Edinburgh, 1968-1972), and he taught economics for 37 years on the Jordanstown campus of the University of Ulster (UU), near Belfast. Awarded a PhD by UU in 1998, he published the thesis in a book, "Valuing Health in Practice" (Routledge 2002), and contributed a chapter to "The Art and Science of Healthcare" (ed. Kirkcaldy Hogrefe 2011). As placement tutor for economics at UU, he helped to develop research at the annual conferences of ASET*, and was made an Honorary member of the Association in 2012. He has published poetry, and has also published in health economics and computing journals, as well as writing for the UK and Irish health services.

*ASET, The Work Based and Placement Learning Association aset@asetonline.org

CONTENTS

Introduction – the context ix

Sam Johnson's Boozers 1
The Meaning Of Meaning: Ken Saro-Wiwa 3
Making It 7
The Assessment Of Teaching 9
We Free Rich At Work 11
The Savage Managers Bear Witnesses 13
Forty Something One Day Down 15
Colourful Natives, Singing 17
Making Peace In Our Time 19
Peace In Our Time 21
Old Lady At The Peace People Assembly 23
Remember Corrymeela? 25
Corrymeela, 3 a.m. 27
The Multiplication Of The Pastors 29
The (Third) Way, The Truth And Your Life 31
Nation Building 35

In Conclusion 37
Basic Reading 39

INTRODUCTION – THE CONTEXT

Across the world, every autumn, thousands of young people leave their homes to study at a university, and, then, to find work in a city. Most expect to avoid cruelly hard work, with the plough, the spade, or the loom, and to find congenial work, in the air-conditioned office, at meetings, or writing reports. Then there are all the young people who will not make it to college, for one reason or another (usually, poverty). But all of you need learning and understanding, and some of it can come from writing your own poetry, or reading others'.

Call my poems candles in the wind, which have illuminated my life, and others' too, and may do the same for yours, as we all face up to the realities of our situations and societies. Seeing what is true, in our corner of civilisation, may be more useful to us, and more easily communicated, than creating or analysing verses which conform to the values of a particular culture.

Bring your critical faculties to bear on my poetry – ask yourself, what is true in these poems, and what is not? And learn thereby.

SAM JOHNSON'S BOOZERS

There is no end to the liquor of knowledge,
Here is infinity, drink what you will;
To know what you are is to tremble, and courage
To stand, reach out, and swallow your fill.

"Let the world go to hell, it was never worth saving,
A ball of clay mud on a galaxy's rump"
But we stay, watch for daybreak, and our offsprings' first gleaming,
Red briars flower by cans on a dump.

Never give up - if you choke, keep on drinking -
Though visions torment, and other vices are wry;
Sam Johnson's boozers see clear in the morning,
Though the cup of their liquor will never run dry.

[Published in *The Belfast Review,* Issue no. 2 Spring 1983]

THE MEANING OF MEANING: KEN SARO-WIWA

Somewhere, a man is in prison.
He did not steal,
Though we cannot imagine the meanings of his poverty.
He did not kill,
Though corruption stinks the whole of his country.
He wrote a poem about freedom and justice, and read it to friends.

When the police beat him,
We do not hear;
His cries and his poem might as well not be,
Like his wife and children,
Though they cry, too.

There is absolutely nothing you can do for him,
Until Amnesty knows, and, it may be, not even then.

In the mean meantime,
Let us open our speech;
Cells of solitary meaning intrigue,
But no-one lives there by choice.

Regardless of cachet or literary status,
However awkward our efforts,
For once, freely, please, honestly available to all,
As close as we can painstakingly come,
The truth.

Let us "alter the lives of the entire country",
Be combative, include politics, economics, you know, everything,
Enter the lives of all of us, and make the spirit matter;
Let us physically endow our words with force and body,
By "living others' lives that they may emulate",
As if we were true writers,
In the manner of *Ken Saro-Wiwa*.

Interview with Ken Saro-Wiwa, reported in *The Independent*, 14/11/95.

"In this country [UK] writers write to entertain, they raise questions of individual existence - you know, the angst of the individual - but for a Nigerian writer in my position you can't go into that. Literature has to be combative. You cannot have art for art's sake. This art must do something to transform the lives of a community, of a nation. And for that reason, literature has a different sort of purpose altogether in that sort of society, completely different from here. And, you know, a writer does not earn money in Nigeria because although you have 100 million people, most of them cannot read and write*, so literature has a different purpose. So here I am - I have written 22 books, I have produced 150 episodes of one television programme, which everyone enjoys, but I am poor. It is of no interest to me. What is of interest to me is that my art should be able to alter the lives of a large number of people, of a whole community, of the entire country, so that my literature has to be entirely different. The stories that I tell must have a different sort of purpose from the artist in the Western world, and it is not now an ego trip, you know, it is politics, it is economics, it's everything, you know, and art, in that instance becomes so meaningful both to the artist and to the consumers of that art, because you do not just depend on them to read your books, you even have to live their life that they can emulate. The artist in that society has a different role, and, to my mind, a much more worthy role than the artist in the West."

Ken Saro-Wiwa was executed by the government of Nigeria on 10th November, 1995. It is no consolation, but *the Nigerian literacy rate, now, is around 60%, and Nigerians are publishing their books on global markets,

MAKING IT

When I arose, and leaped to meet its gaze,
A summer's glorious, energizing sun,
They said: "Your life must prove itself in these few days,
Or else be nothing when the race is won."
So sieze the time, when years are flown so fast,
Build a lasting work against all spite -
How shall we move before our lives are passed,
How shall we build our stairway to the light?
Alone, each knows no path but that he treads,
Apart, each hears no song but that he sings,
   -   So we unite, in mobs our fears to shed,
And willing, yet unwilling, make our kings.
But each one sleeps uneasy, muttering,
And our meagre rushlights waver, guttering.

[Published in the Spring 2009 issue of *Reflexion,* a University of Ulster magazine]

THE ASSESSMENT OF TEACHING

In the journals they ask:
How may we properly (academically) (rationally)
Measure some One? (Promotion-wise)
The professional guardians of our children's minds
Grade and school and teach educationally,
With the best of intentions and evidence for their methods,
Under orders.

Meanwhile, inside the pupil and outside the classroom,
Lives roll on their ruts.
Properly then, (for the changing of lives),
What criteria?
When people re-define what is possible,
When they break out of their shells,
And painfully, joyfully, dis-cover,
When they continually deliver the unexpected and the original,
Without rational cause, but in harmony and with their reason -
I'd say you were probably doing something right.

So much of our teaching is mis-taken.

"Reality" now rules - forever and ever?
One day, we'll see men and women bursting from their cages,
Letting go their rages, and finally
Trusting themselves, as no-one else would,
To find their own futures.

The force-feeding of artificial learning to children
Makes tortured ignorant adults,
And a society of bullies.

Criticism's the kindest cut – where is it?
Indifference is the cruellest – it's everywhere!
And false praise murders wisdom.

UK state education was established in 1946, with the aim of providing to all the opportunities which had only been available to the wealthy, or to scholarship winners. It was not based on democratic principles, of what society as a whole needed its people to know and understand, but on the imitation of "best practice" of the schools already in existence. Over the last sixty years, fundamental change has become long overdue, though many people of goodwill make huge efforts to keep the system working.

WE FREE RICH AT WORK

We are not restricted by our separate cells;

Nor are the walls patrolled by any guard

But our own interest. Safe, we freely sport ourselves

With loud and varied noise; if times are hard,

Why, we complain, and if by chance they're fine,

Then we will celebrate, fulfil our ages,

This multi-story life is heady wine,

And we ignore the paced confinement of our cages.

Responsible authority? Us? You may well grin,

For here's a breach observed by states, in need

Of custom strong – our lives do want holding in,

We're caged by our own self-interested prosperity,

And no-one dares destroy the walls of insecurity.

THE SAVAGE MANAGERS BEAR WITNESSES

Each defends a patch and a pack;
In agonies of conscience and uncertainty,
They secure control on a daily basis;
Never secure, never content.

The law of nature is their rule book,
"What works" and "reality" are their watch words;
They freely choose to desire, in every minute of life,
Those corporate objectives.

Abandoning free will, they get their deserts.

To get there, these brutes have beaten down,
Subjugated, imprisoned, forced to bow
In countless meaningless but demeaning ways
The human beings, the decent people.

Some capitulate at once, with a sigh
Of lamentation. Who shall blame?
Others struggle to resist,
And sacrifice - illusions, mainly,
About freedom, justice, and their co-workers.

Pulled away from true North by these brutes' force,
Eventually or quickly they give in,
Illusion-free, they sleep soundly,
And know themselves, and others,
Better.

The magnetic field is still there,
And will not be wished away by the savages managing.

Let your example make the forces of nature visible,
Help us all to see the kindness we expect,
At the heart of all workplaces.

FORTY SOMETHING ONE DAY DOWN

"Life's a bitch and then you're dead"
She said, as if there were no echoes,
No memories, no heavens and no hells,
Here or elsewhere,
As if examples did not reverbrate,
Broadcast all around, seeds for the future,
Whether she likes it or not,
To tint our common heavens grey or blue.

She wasn't deprived, in fact the cream she was,
Among the brightest, God help us,
And, I have no doubt, a "realist",
Who thought the truth would make her free.

It's true; free she is,
Like water without a bucket or a gardener.

COLOURFUL NATIVES, SINGING

We, the clever rich white men, once
Were colourful natives, singing,
Contented round our own hearthstones.

We have since followed our cleverness elsewhere,
Made a chieftain of Progress,
And slowly infected the spleen of mankind.

To-day in the lives of the poor coloured peoples,
We recognise the universal trades -
Purity for colour,
Current acceptance for birthright,
To-morrow's trash for to-day's dreams.

The song of Progress is a knell for the world,
"No homeland, no birthright, no family."

This death would serve no purpose.

Let us all be natives again,
But of one family, one village, and one country,
With one new colourful universal song,
Enacted every day in peace:

"Homeland is our birthright,
Humanity is our family,
And One God is our Parent."

Sing our song,
And let living be coloured again,
Ringing and singing with harmony,
Through all the hills, valleys, and plains of the Earth,
Our Eden.

MAKING PEACE IN OUR TIME

Remember our great wars, and in detail;
Our fighting fathers knew not what they did -
Come to forgive, but remember, every one,
Their barbaric acts of war.

The hurting for and taking of revenge
Defeats the takers, like spit in the wind;
Our fathers knew not what they did -
Forgive and remember, "obeying orders" does not excuse
Barbaric acts of war.

In the soil of remembrance
Plant the acorns of peace;
Water them well, every day, for years,
With the deliberate endless tears
Of for-giving, and giving, and giving,
The pain and sorrow wrung out of your soul.

It may be no consolation at all,
But these oaks could burst the prisons,
Crumble the foundations of hatred,
And set us all free.

Not peace in our time,
But peace in our children's time,
If they need not forgive and remember
Our own barbaric acts of war.

PEACE IN OUR TIME
[Written before the Berlin Wall came down, and shortly before the first Northern Ireland ceasefire, which began on August 31, 1994.]

When you walk the ordinary streets of Belfast,
And see the people go about their business,
You'll think, it's like a normal city.
If you see the troops and guns,
Watch the armoured cars and the barracks,
You'll feel, this is no normal place.

When you stride the long avenues of Paris,
And feel their ancient soothing charms,
You'll know an intermittent sense of peace.
If you hear the terrorists' bomb,
Watch the armoured cops and the ambulances,
Paris will not be normal.

When you promenade the strasse of Berlin,
And smell the wealth in the Western windows,
You'll think, what a normal smell.
If you hear the Wall's sirens,
Watch the armoured cars and the goons,
You'll know Berlin's a Cold War battlefield.

When you step out brave along the Falls,
And feel a thrilling touch of real fear,
You'll know again it's good to be alive.
If you see ordinary people defenceless,
Watch the commonplace background to violence,
Normal, wherever you're from,
Will not be Home.

[Published in the 7th September 1984 issue of *Peace by Peace,* a magazine produced by the Peace People]

OLD LADY AT THE PEACE PEOPLE ASSEMBLY

She doesn't look implacable, or resolute;
She smiles, often, as if she could be shaken,
As if she could be satisfied;
But nothing less than peace,
Nothing less than the Kingdom of God,
Will placate this old and iron maiden,
Whose resolve will conquer,
Whose love will never die,
Whose actions speak quietly and firmly,
Without rebuke.

There are no flowers
For your average committee member,
No mindless roars of media adulation
For your OAP lover and peaceworker.
Virtue is its own reward,
And meagre it is, for most of us.
But she doggedly, implacably, and mysteriously
Continues to serve our peace.

Her resolve will conquer in the end,
Her love will never die;
Hear her actions, every one,
Small noise though they are,
In the muffled silence of our community's fear.

REMEMBER CORRYMEELA?

(Corrymeela is a place (the Centre overlooking the sea near Ballycastle), and it is a group of people working for peace in Northern Ireland, with members all over the island, and in the UK, of different religions and none.)

Everyone was there, all the important people,
From every condition and age,
On an island, together,
Among the windswept sea and sky at Ballycastle.

Our week was not always fun,
(Though often fun sparkled, rippling and beautiful
As if life was easy)
It was like being in love, or being in a good family,
Full to the brim of everything worthwhile,
From the poor, the rich, the sick, and the well,
The single, the wedded, the old, and the very young,
And (not forgetting) ould God,
They all were there.

God wasn't a stranger to any of us,
But the pushes and pulls of the family life
Eased off the scales, the survival shellac layers,
That in the everyday keep us from Him.

[Published in the October 1982 issue of *Corrymeela News*]

CORRYMEELA, 3 A.M.

No, we are not playing games, for
The continual chatter makes a difference -
Our sudden sparks give light,
To disconnected streets,
When rules are gone.

Yes, the pain is real, for
Sufferings rise to new friends' faces,
From the unknown deeps of unaware glances -
Many times, we're afraid to touch these sores,
Doubting our caring.

Lord, give us eyes to see pain clearly,
Wisdom and caring to heal strangers humbly,
And faith, to go the whole dreadful thorny length of love,
For their sakes, ours, and yours,
Amen.

THE MULTIPLICATION OF THE PASTORS

Church is OUT;
Far and wide the seeds fly, wild, winged, and wounded,
On stony soil and concrete, fertile ground, and the sea -
Shifts are made, some growth can be seen,
And some of us just drown.

In the husks there are echoes,
And the odd seed is left, unflown,
To root in clammy sepulchres,
Without the sun.

Rooting and growing, our DNA does the structure;
We have the program, human,
As in god's image,
Making tracks towards heaven,
Alone and together, in the true faith of our fathers,
That we are truly one,
And that God gives a damn.

No-one can separate us but ourselves,
We have the wherewithal,
To survive, to thrive,
And build the shining city on a hill.

Pastor: This means YOU. And me, too.

THE (THIRD) WAY, THE TRUTH AND YOUR LIFE

How powerless the politicians are!
In every part of life,
Lives roll on their ruts, the poor and sick still suffer,
And the wicked wage their strife,
Breaking the assumptions of due process
With a will and a way, inspired, every day,
By the media's rich populist panders.

As the government would say if it had the guts,
"We really can't control that much,
Can't sack our servants or sue them,
(And you can't get good help these days)
It's all too complicated,
Do you know how much paperwork
A Cabinet minister gets through?
Sorry, but you're on your own;
Whatever you do, don't live in a place that's rundown,
Avoid going to law, and be nice to everyone,
Especially the wicked.
Oh, and don't expect the spirit of the law,
(That we were elected to deliver),

Just the letter, always assuming we voted enough money
To get the drafting right."

In every language except plain English,
They say we're on our own - we owe them no respect,
Except as the best manipulators in the land,
Or the most promising compromising people
Any one could find anywhere,
Who can live with contradictions so easily -
No princesses, they are comfy on a fakir's bed of nails,
The secret is, "not minding".
Well, I mind, and I tell you,
God is not mocked;
Believe in Him, accept His justice,
And pray for his mercy.

The harm the wicked do is finely judged,
To lie within the letter of the law;
Their public reputation's never smudged,
By outright wrong that one might say (in court) he saw.
But God is not mocked;
Believe in Him, accept His justice,
And pray for his mercy.

His writ runs now and here, through every aspect of our lives,
"N-tuple" entry book-keeping, where
"N" is a large number, balance is kept,
Between spirit and wealth, virtue and health,
Un-measurable and undetectable,
Because he is God, and we are his.

Hard to believe,
But how many ways we suffer and differ,
How many ways we strive and live,
How hard to define "happiness",
And how ignorant we are about ourselves and those we love.

Makes you feel small, doesn't it?
Perhaps we all are,
From the Prime Minister down,
Or from the Prime Minister, up.

NATION BUILDING

"Your accent is Scottish, are you?

It was not clear just what he meant,
What expectations he had formed
Of my internal forces' resolution –
Should he keep his guard up,
Stiff and fierce against a (headstrong) Celt,
Or even seek the vulnerable spot,
Between the sporran and the belt –
Hence "below the belt", coined in Border fights,
 -   If you must know, nothing's worn beneath the kilt,
Except flesh-tinted tights, long johns,
And a precious chip off the shoulder,
Hidden where no-one would want to look.

I'm sure I'm still a mystery to him; he is, to me.

From the local garrison towers,
The birthrights wave their flags,
Scarred all over, with wounds from long ago,
Desperate, and ready to weep blood like rain,
For sheer redress and solidarity.

In fact, we are free to choose our own public histories;
Uniforms (corroded), battles (bloody), value judgements (tattered)
Mistakes, and other commitments (gun-shaped),
There are plenty to choose from.

If our minds met, we could make one public common history,
Known, at least, to each other, and understood.

But is there anything to keep the rain out?
Or sustain your force for good over a life-time,
Or (even) save the planet?

My own people's daily informal Christianity
Is the best of my inheritance;
It's showerproof, though you have to keep mending,
But not yet warm, or comforting.

From the commitments we choose in our freedom,
We can make our common mystery nation;
Let's see who we are, and who, together, we can become.

IN CONCLUSION

My generation has had its turn. It's your world now, mend it, make it better, work hard, and we'll have our Eden. Here. Now (well, maybe the day after tomorrow).

With kindest wishes, and great respect (you are the future),

Douglas

BASIC READING
– what you don't know *can* hurt you.

Bryson Bill *A Short History of Nearly Everything* Black Swan (2016)

Davidson B *The Black Man's Burden - Africa and the Curse of the Nation State* (1992)

Goldacre Ben *Bad Science* Fourth Estate (2009)

Hawken Paul (ed) *Drawdown: The Most Comprehensive Plan Ever Proposed to Reverse Global Warming* Penguin (2018)

Jordan D and Walsh M *White Cargo – the forgotten history of Britain's White Slaves in America* Mainstream Publishing (2007)

McGee Thomas D'Arcy *A Popular History of Ireland – from the Earliest Period to the Emancipation of the Catholics (Complete) A Public Domain Book.* (Free on Amazon Kindle)

Milton Keynes UK
Ingram Content Group UK Ltd.
UKHW030749230724
445892UK00003B/71